Let's get pawsitive!

Welcome! This workbook is intended to be used with *Be as Happy as Your Dog: 16 Dog-Tested Ways to Be Happier Using Pawsitive Psychology* by Michelle Waitzman. If you haven't read that book, I recommend at least starting it before you use this workbook, since it will make much more sense when you use them together.

Be as Happy as Your Dog is a self-help book that explains how you can learn to enjoy life like dogs do. By bringing together the latest research from dog behavior experts and leaders in positive psychology, the book reveals easy changes you can make to level up your happiness today—and make it last.

Each section of the workbook is based on one chapter of the book, and one "dog-tested way to be happier." You can either read the whole book and then begin the exercises in the workbook, or you can go chapter-by-chapter, completing each section of the workbook after you finish reading the corresponding chapter in the book. You can read the chapters in any order you like!

The exercises in this workbook are based on positive (or pawsitive) psychology, a field of research that helps everyone—regardless of their starting point or circumstances—to lead a happier, more fulfilling life and increase their sense of well-being.

You might want to keep some extra sheets of paper or a notebook handy while you are using this workbook, in case you want to write down longer answers for some of the exercises than you can fit in the space provided.

Using these exercises will help you make your life a bit happier every day!

Stay pawsitive!

Michelle Waitzman

Be as Happy as Your Dog
1. Learn new tricks

A "new trick" is any new skill or habit that will improve your life and make you happier. It could be an exercise habit, a new way of eating, a new interest or hobby—just about anything!

Brainstorm

List the new tricks you want to learn or adopt. Then describe how each one could make you happier

New trick		Why it would make me happier
1.	🐾	
2.	🐾	
3.	🐾	
4.	🐾	
5.	🐾	
6.	🐾	

Pick your trick

What are the three new tricks that would make the biggest difference to your long-term happiness?

1. _____

2. _____

3. _____

Pick the trick you're going to start learning right away. What steps will you take, starting today, to learn your new habit or skill

New trick:

Step 1: _____

Step 2: _____

Step 3: _____

Step 4: _____

Step 5: _____

Step 6: _____

Don't wait for the "right time" to start something new. Start right away and give yourself time to become good at it.

Track your milestones

Milestone	Date	Results

Reflect

Has learning this new trick added more happiness to your life? In what ways?

_____

_____

_____

_____

_____

Repeat this process with more of your new tricks!

2. Live in the moment

People spend about half their time thinking either about the past or the future. Bringing your attention back to the present moment gives you more opportunities to be happy throughout the day.

What's on your mind?

1. List all of the things you're worried or anxious about that are distracting you from the present moment. (Use a separate sheet if you need to.)

2. After completing your list, put an "X" beside the things that are out of your control or that you can't do anything about right away. Try to be aware when those things come to mind and set aside those thoughts to refocus on what's happening right now.

X

Where does the day go?

List the things you do daily (or regularly) without giving them much thought.

Practicing mindfulness

Choose an item from the list above and start paying more attention to the experience the next time you do it.

Now that you've paid more attention to your activity, answer these questions below:

* ❀ What was unique about the experience today?
  * ❀ What about this activity am I grateful for?
* ❀ How can this activity add happiness to my day?
  * ❀ How could I improve how I do this activity to enjoy or appreciate it more?

Use a notebook or document to write down these observations for the other activities you listed.

Be happy right now. Each new moment presents you with the possibility of happiness, and it's up to you to gratefully embrace it.

Take time to savor

Choose something to savor today. It could be a food, activity, or environment. Go through all the stages below and reflect on the experience. Try to experience it as if it's your first time.

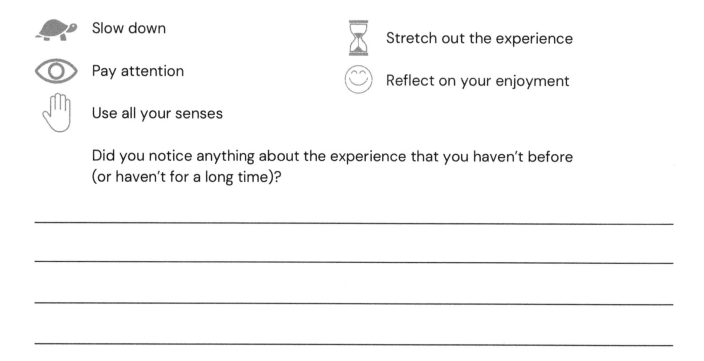

Slow down

Pay attention

Use all your senses

Stretch out the experience

Reflect on your enjoyment

Did you notice anything about the experience that you haven't before (or haven't for a long time)?

_____

_____

_____

_____

Quiet your mind

Schedule a period of time today to meditate, or quiet your mind. This could be anywhere from 5 minutes to 30 minutes—however long you can stay still and focused. Choose a method that you're comfortable with. Here are some suggestions:

∞ guided meditations (apps or videos),
∞ listening to calming sounds,
∞ sitting quietly and focusing on calming and emptying your mind, or
∞ any other meditation practice you've learned.

| Time | Place | Method |

After you finish, write down a few thoughts on how you felt and whether you want to do something differently tomorrow. Repeat daily in a journal or notebook.

Day 1

_____

_____

_____

Day 2

_____

_____

_____

Day 3

_____

_____

_____

Day 4

_____

_____

_____

Dogs enjoy every belly rub, meal, walk, and opportunity to play. If we look at our lives as a string of mostly positive events and enjoy them as they unfold, we set ourselves up for greater happiness.

3. Wag your tail

Celebrate and share your happy moments with the people (and dogs) around you more often. This will add more happiness to both your life and theirs!

How are you celebrating?

Who you "wag your tail" with and how you do it might change depending on what you're happy about. You could involve your spouse or partner, workmates, teammates, friends, extended family, kids, pets, classmates, or anyone you interact with. Celebrating could involve:

- posting on social media
- sending a message or email
- phoning someone
- chatting in person
- going out to celebrate
- sharing a meal or treat
- capturing the moment in a photo

Other ideas:

Save up your wins

Start documenting all the good things that happen every day by writing them on slips of paper that you add to a jar or a decorated box. At the end of the year, open the container and read the slips to appreciate how many great things you experienced.

Share your joy with all the world by wagging your tail. Why hide your happiness when you can spread it to everyone?

Celebrate everything

Brainstorm ideas about what you could do to celebrate and who you could do it with. I've started with a few areas where you might have "wins" to celebrate, but you should add your own.

Type of win	Who to celebrate with and how
Work	
Health	
Relationship	
New habit	

Celebrate without working for it

Celebrate good things that happen to you (or others) even if you didn't do anything to help make them happen! Notice all the good things that life puts in your path.

Good things that happened today ...	How I celebrated
To me:	
To someone I know:	
Around me:	
In the world:	

Use the table above as a guideline for a journal. Make two columns on each page—one to list your wins, and the other to write down how you celebrated them and who you celebrated with. Fill it in every evening to capture all the ways you "wag your tail" and think about how you could add more of them every day.

4. Never stop playing

Playing throughout our lives is essential for good physical and mental health. It helps to boost productivity and creativity, prevent depression and dementia, and much more. Plus, it's fun!

Play your way

Often, the games and activities you enjoyed the most when you were a child provide insight into the ways you prefer to play. Take a moment to think back and write down some of your favorite childhood activities.

Thinking about both the activities you listed, and the things that you do for fun now, circle the play styles that best describe you. You may identify strongly with just one or you may enjoy several styles.

Play Style*	Description
Joker	You like to goof around and play practical jokes
Kinesthete	You never sit still, and you think better when you're moving
Explorer	You crave physical or mental exploration
Competitor	You love to keep score and always try to win
Director	You enjoy planning and executing activities and you're always organizing things
Collector	You enjoy collecting and categorizing things or ticking items off your bucket list
Artist/Creator	You enjoy art, crafts, cooking, or tinkering
Storyteller	You enjoy writing or creating a narrative to motivate your activities

*These play styles are based on the work of Dr. Stuart Brown of the National Institute for Play.

Have more fun

Looking at your play personality results, list the activities you do now that align with your preferences.

Play Style   Activity

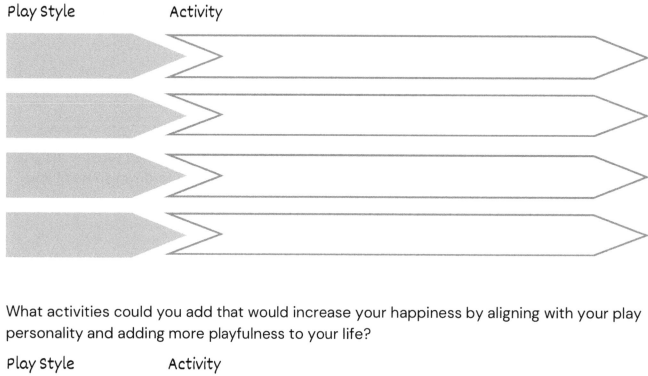

What activities could you add that would increase your happiness by aligning with your play personality and adding more playfulness to your life?

Play Style   Activity

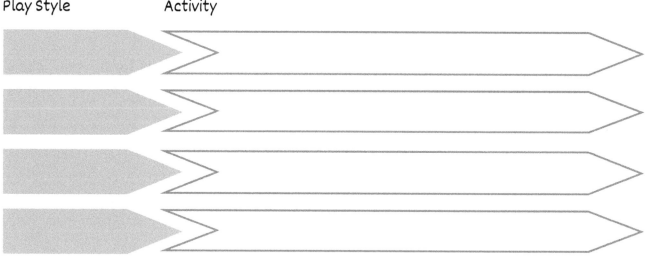

Playing is an expression of pure happiness because it lets you enjoy things just for the sake of enjoying them.

Choose your playmates

Who would be the best people to ask to join you in your new play activities? These could even be people you don't know yet, like members of a sports league or art class.

Activity   Person/people to do it with

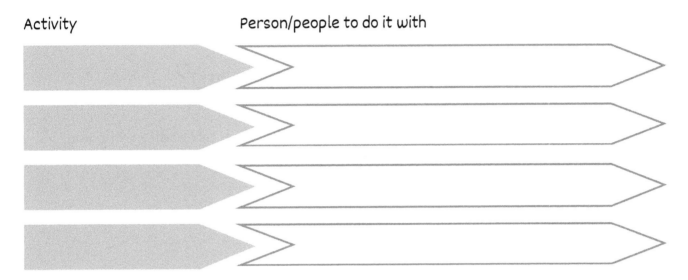

Schedule your play

Now that you know what you want to do and who you want to do it with, find the times in your schedule(s) when you can add these. Remember to prioritize play, even if it means moving some other commitments to a new time or day.

Activity   Dates & times

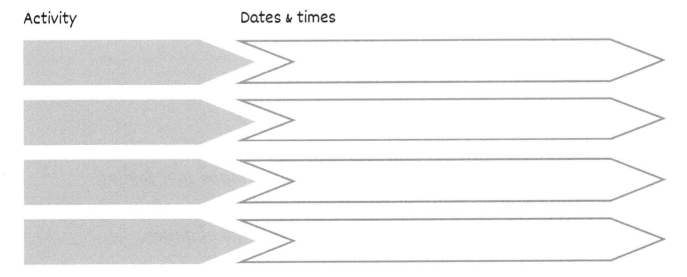

5. Find your pack

Surrounding yourself with a few supportive, positive people who always have your back will make it much easier to become and stay happy.

Who is in your pack now?

Name the people you're currently closest to. The ones you see or talk to often, who you confide in, and who know you the best. For each of them, write down:

1. Their relationship to you
2. What you talk about often when you're together
3. How you tend to feel after spending time with them

Add more names below or on another sheet if you need to.

Name
1.
2.
3.

Name
1.
2.
3.

Me

Name
1.
2.
3.

Name
1.
2.
3.

Spending time around your pack should leave you feeling refreshed and happy. If you are not getting this result, you may need to think about making some changes.

Rate your pack

Consider people in your life who make you feel happy, confident, calm, and positive. What are the things you discuss or do together that make this true?

Now consider the pack members who make you feel guilty, frustrated, angry, not good enough, and negative. What are the things you talk about or do together that make this true?

Know your pack strenths

Think about how you interact with the people in your pack and what their individual strengths and weaknesses are. Complete the following statements:

The best person to tell when something good happens is   because

_____

The best person to tell when something bad happens is   because

_____

The person who gives me the most support is   because

_____

The person I give the most support to is   because

_____

The person I laugh with the most is   because

_____

The person I trust the most is   because

_____

The person I can really be myself with is   because

_____

Is there anyone you would like to spend less time with or remove from your pack?

Is there anyone you would like to spend more time with or add to your pack?

6. Trust the "sniff test"

Understanding your instant reactions to new people and honing your skills at reading their signals can help you become happier by avoiding people you don't "click" with and knowing why you dislike them.

Do you use your sniff test?

On a scale of 0–5 (0 being never, and 5 being always), how much do the following statements apply to you:

Score

1. I can tell immediately whether a person is nice or not.

2. I trust my intuition without question because it is very reliable.

3. I can tell when someone is lying to me.

4. I bond with new friends very quickly.

5. When someone makes me uncomfortable, I cut them out of my life if I can.

6. I know when something is bothering my friends and loved ones, even if they don't tell me.

If you scored higher than 20 in total, you trust your "sniff test" quite a lot. If you scored under 15, you are skeptical about yours.

Assess your sniffing skills

Write down the name (or description) of someone you recently met for the first time.

_____

Try to remember your first impression of that person, and your initial interaction. Answer the questions on the next page without thinking too hard about it or analyzing your first thoughts.

Did you like them?

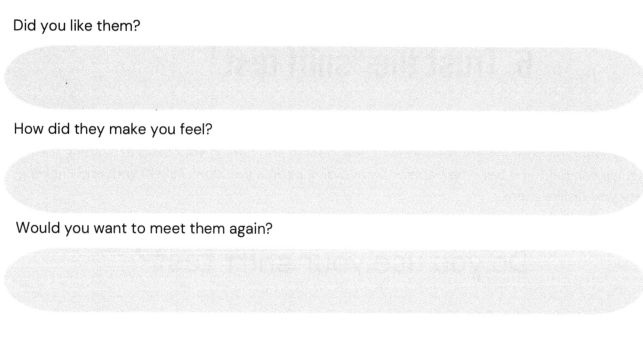

How did they make you feel?

Would you want to meet them again?

Thinking back about your interaction, try to list 3-5 things that influenced your answers to those questions.

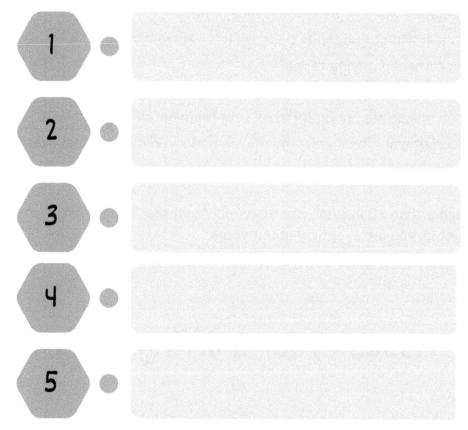

1

2

3

4

5

Just like dogs, we humans have a like-o-meter too, and it's always running.

Improve your sniffing

What do you notice first when you meet someone new?

Have you made assumptions about a new person (positive or negative) based on your first impression that later turned out to be wrong? What were they? Why did you assume those things about them? (Use another sheet if you need to.)

What could you pay more attention to when you meet someone to help you decide how you feel about them?

If someone fails your "sniff test," what will you do about it?

7. Bark, don't bite

It's easier to resolve upsetting situations when you deal with them early on. As time passes and you get more upset, you are more likely to "bite" by reacting with an outburst of anger.

What makes you growly?

1. Using the table below, list the things that you have been feeling angry, frustrated, or irritated about lately. Be as specific as possible about what is bothering you. For example, instead of just listing "my in-laws" get more specific, such as "my in-laws show up uninvited and without warning." Use another sheet if you have a lot to list.

2. Now think about who you need to talk to (or bark at) to get each issue resolved. This could include the people directly involved (like your in-laws) and people who might be able to intervene on your behalf if you explain the situation to them (like your spouse).

Issue	Who could help resolve it

Prepare to bark

List the issues again, and this time write down the key points you need to get across in order to resolve the issue. This will help you to stay focused on the exact issue you want to resolve, instead of having a wide-ranging argument that will likely just upset you both further.

Remember to make your key points about solutions rather than accusations. State the problem and how you would like to solve it with the other person's (or people's) help.

Issue	Key points

Track your results

How did your discussions go? Keep track of your results here or use another sheet if you need more space.

If you didn't resolve the issue, check whether you need to adjust your key points. Are you asking for the right things? Are you asking in a way that the other person (or people) might accept? Cross off an issue when it has been completely resolved.

Issue	Discussion date	Results

Standing up for yourself is a form of self-care and self-respect. Making other people happy at your own expense will eventually make you less capable of caring for them.

8. Shake it off

What you do with your body can influence your thoughts and emotions. If negative thoughts are weighing you down, you can shake them off like a dog.

shake things up

What are some of the things that happen regularly in your life that you find frustrating or irritating? Do they ruin your whole day? Write down some of these annoying events that are stealing your happiness for longer than necessary.

_____

_____

_____

_____

_____

The next time you experience one of these, try not to let it stay with you all day. Instead, as soon as the moment has passed, take a few deep breaths and try to let it go. If that doesn't work, try one of the other "shake it off" suggestions in the next section.

> *Whenever dogs shake, they are basically resetting their mood back to neutral and getting ready to move on to to something new—they are basically saying "Well, that's over. What's next?"*

Choose your shake-up

Try some of the methods below when you need to reset your mood from negative to positive.

Experiment and see which methods of shaking it off are most effective for you. Some might work at certain times, but require too much time and effort at other times. Keep track of how you feel after trying different activities to discover your best shakes!

I've listed some of the methods from **Be as Happy as Your Dog**, but I've also left some blank rows where you can add your own ideas.

Method	How well did it work?
Take deep breaths	
Stretch	
Go for a walk	
Ask a friend to cheer you up	
Exercise	
Go forest bathing (visit nature)	
Watch something you enjoy	
Listen to feel-good music	

Learn from the past

There are probably some events from your past that still bother you sometimes, even though there's nothing you can do to change them now. You might still feel angry, bitter, or embarrassed by them every time they pop into your mind.

1. List the past experiences that you are still carrying with you that make you unhappy.
2. Try to look at them from a "lessons learned" perspective. What has that experience taught you that could help you avoid a similar outcome if it happened again?
3. When these events pop into your mind again, focus on what you learned, and feel confident that you can handle any similar situation that you are faced with. There is nothing to feel anxious or bitter about.

What happened	What I learned from it

Getting outside more often and adding more physical activity to your life are important ingredients in the recipe for happiness.

Take stock of your activities

Write down all the outdoor activities and physical activities you regularly participate in, and when you do them. Dog walking counts, but not if it's just a quick potty break.

Monday	Tuesday	Wednesday

Thursday	Friday	Saturday
		Sunday

Make a plan

Are there activities in your current schedule you could do more often? Or different activities you would enjoy doing that you haven't yet found time for? It's important to choose activities you actually enjoy, or you'll find excuses not to do them.

What are the times and days when you could add an activity? Think about your mornings, lunch breaks, after work, after dinner, etc.

List some activities you would like to add to your schedule so that you are active every day. Match the activities you'd like to add to your routine to the times when they might fit into your schedule.

Mark your activities with "C" for current activities and "N" for new activities.

Activity		Days & times

Find a buddy

For your current and future activities, who could be your "accountability buddy" to make sure you're sticking to your plans? It could be a person who does the activity with you, or just someone who will check in to see if you did it as planned.

Activity	Buddy

Your dog doesn't care how far they get on their walk, or how many calories they burn. They're just happy to be on the go with their human, enjoying the journey. This is the highlight of their day!

Be as Happy as Your Dog
10. Stop and smell things

You can find more moments of happiness every day by taking the time to give your full attention to what's happening around you.

Turn off your "autopilot"

Think of activities you go through every day on "autopilot" without paying much attention. Write them below and add ways you could refocus your attention on them by engaging your senses.

Activity	How to focus on it

Reflect on your experiences

Choose a day of the week to focus on each of the activities in your list. On that day, make a point of focusing your attention on that activity and appreciating the experience of doing it.

In the spaces below, write down what you noticed while you focused on the activity that you would normally have ignored or missed completely. Use a blank sheet to add more activities.

Activity:

Observations:

Activity:

Observations:

Activity:

Observations:

Activity:

Observations:

Practice being observant

Using a small notebook or the voice recorder on your phone, make a note every time you see or experience something good during your day. At the end of the day, look at (or listen to) your list of positive things you experienced that day.

* How many positive experiences are you having every day?
* Is it more than you expected?
* Does writing them down or talking about them make them seem more important?
* What have you discovered about your daily experiences by doing this?

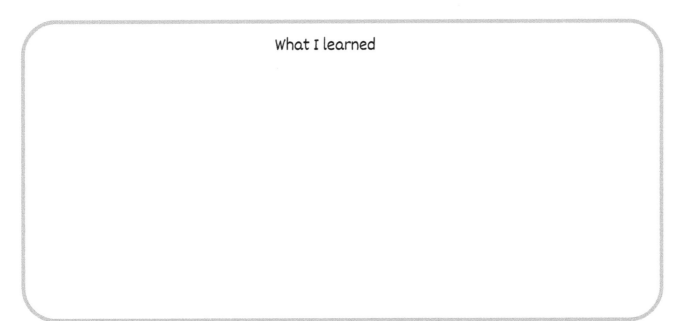

What I learned

Invite serendipity

Choose a week to experiment with being more open to changing your plans when new opportunities come up. This will leave you open to serendipity—the possibility of finding something that is even better than what you were seeking or planning.

Using the spaces on the next page, at the end of each day, write down what you did that wasn't part of your original plan for the day, and whether it made you happy.

Unplanned activities & happiness results

Monday

Tuesday

Wednesday

Thursday

Friday

Saturday

Sunday

Did being open to more serendipity result in more positive experiences and happiness overall? How could you use serendipity to be happier?

Of all the gifts you can give, your attention is perhaps the greatest of all.

11. Enjoy some treats

A treat is "an event or item that is out of the ordinary and gives great pleasure." It doesn't have to be something you earn or deserve (or eat).

What are your non-edible treats?

Treats don't always have to be food (although there's nothing wrong with enjoying food treats). List 10 treats you could give yourself that don't involve food.

1. _____

2. _____

3. _____

4. _____

5. _____

6. _____

7. _____

8. _____

9. _____

10. _____

Are you withholding treats?

Describe a time when you denied yourself a treat because you didn't feel like you had "earned" it yet. Did you eventually give yourself the treat? Did you still want it and enjoy it? Would you have accomplished your goal without withholding the treat?

Use the "worth it" test

List some of treats you have most often, and some that you rarely have.
- How much pleasure do you get from each of them?
- What are the negative consequences of indulging in that treat (if any)?

If the pleasure outweighs the consequences, put a √ in the "worth it" column and keep enjoying that treat on occasion. If the consequences outweigh the pleasure you get from the treat, put a x in the "worth it" column and stop using that particular treat.

This can become your guide to choosing treats when you want one.

Treat	Worth it?	Treat	Worth it?

Is it still a treat?

Are there any treats you have habitually? For example, every time you work out, every week on the same day, or every time you get together with certain friends?

When you automatically have a treat after a certain trigger, it stops being a treat and becomes a habit or an expectation instead.

List the treats that have become habits or expectations, and decide which habits you need to break, and which ones are positive habits that add happiness to your life.

Habitual treat	Keep it or break it?

Unlike dogs, a lot of people believe they should only have treats when they've done something out of the ordinary to deserve them. There is nothing in the definition of "treat" that says they need to be earned or deserved.

12. Accept praise

Many people feel embarrassed by compliments, or automatically put themselves down. Accepting praise when people notice your best qualities and accomplishments can improve your self-esteem and make you happy.

What's great about you?

List the personal attributes you're most proud of. These could be career-related skills and accomplishments, something you bring to your personal relationships, creative or manual skills you've learned, contributions to your community, etc.

1. _____

2. _____

3. _____

4. _____

5. _____

6. _____

7. _____

8. _____

9. _____

10. _____

How do you normally react when someone compliments you on one of these attributes? Do you feel good? Awkward? Do you say something negative about yourself to downplay it?

How could you respond that would make both you and the person who praised you feel comfortable and happy?

Go back to your list. Read each item and then look at yourself in the mirror and praise yourself for it. Do this until you believe you deserve the praise and are ready to hear it from others!

Practice accepting praise

What is your reaction when someone praises you for something—your appearance, your cooking, your work—anything you don't generally think you excel at. Are you pleased or embarrassed ? Why?

How could you change your reaction to become more comfortable with accepting praise for things that you don't expect to be praised for?

Practice praising others

Think about some of the people who have qualities you admire. They could be family, friends, work colleagues, or anyone you interact with regularly. List them below, and then describe what you admire about them.

Name   Praiseworthy qualities

When you next see any of the people on your list, be sure to praise them for one of the qualities you listed (or more than one). Be sincere.

How did each person respond to being praised? Is there anything you can learn from their response about how to deliver sincere praise? Is there anything you can learn about how to accept sincere praise?

Write down these responses and lessons below.

Name		Response to praise
	🐾	
	🐾	
	🐾	
	🐾	
	🐾	
	🐾	
	🐾	
	🐾	
	🐾	

Once you get used to praising others, expand beyond this list of people and give others praise whenever they deserve it. This can include people you don't know at all!

> *Learning to accept praise is important for your happiness because it reinforces positive feelings about yourself. It also encourages you to keep working hard toward your goals because the effort is paying off.*

Be as Happy as Your Dog
13. Play fetch

Chasing after things you want can be inherently satisfying and add happiness to your life. On the other hand, constantly wanting to replace what you have, however great it is, with something new is the wrong way to play fetch.

It's all about the chase

List some of the activities that make you feel really great and excited while you're doing them, regardless of the outcome. These could include creative pursuits, sports, games, physical activities, work-related tasks, and hobbies.

1. _____

2. _____

3. _____

4. _____

5. _____

6. _____

7. _____

8. _____

Do you ever get so immersed in any of these activities that you lose track of time or you're reluctant to stop doing them when you have something else to take care of? Put a star next to those activities. They are the ones that put you in a state of "flow" and will probably make you feel happiest.

Don't get addicted to "new"

List the activities that you do over and over, trying to get the temporary rush you feel from achieving them. These could be things like buying new shoes or clothing, upgrading your phone or other gadgets, landing a new job, dating someone new, etc.

1. _____

2. _____

3. _____

4. _____

5. _____

6. _____

Do any of these activities provide lasting satisfaction, or do you soon want to go searching for something better? Put a "x" next to anything that you quickly get bored with, or that you have accumulated a large number of that you don't use.

These are your "hedonic treadmill" activities—the things you can't seem to stop chasing. They will never bring you real happiness, just momentary pleasure. Avoid relying on these to boost your mood. Instead, focus on the things that provide long-term happiness.

If you participate in your hedonic treadmill activities with the same people all the time, what could you do together to replace this activity and refocuses your attention on enjoying the moment together, rather than just getting "stuff"?

Appreciate what you have

What good things are already part of your life that you could spend more time enjoying and appreciating. How could you do that?

Which of your "flow" activities could you do more of, to get the most happiness and personal growth from them? How can you add more of them to your schedule?

The key to playing fetch is to find joy in the activity itself instead of being happy only when you reach your goal.

Be as Happy as Your Dog
14. Chase the uncatchable

Pursuing big dreams and goals can bring you happiness long before you achieve them. Just remember to enjoy the process and celebrate every step you take.

Your dreams and goals

List your biggest dreams and goals, including your childhood dreams if they still appeal to you. (Don't include things you have no control over, like winning the lottery or being taller.)

Put a check next to the ones you believe would add the most happiness to your life if you achieved them or made progress toward them.

1. _____

2. _____

3. _____

4. _____

5. _____

6. _____

Choose one of these dreams or goals to focus on first. You'll use this to complete the rest of the exercises. It should be something you're willing to work toward for a long time. (You can use additional sheets of paper to do this for your other dreams and goals.)

Dream or goal: _____

Where are you now?

List all of the things you've already done to work toward your goal or dream. (Use another sheet if necessary.) Include any reading, courses, skills, jobs, contacts, plans, or anything else that have put you on a path toward achieving your goal or dream.

1. _____

2. _____

3. _____

4. _____

5. _____

6. _____

7. _____

8. _____

9. _____

10. _____

Are you surprised by how much or how little you've written down? If you've never taken stock of your progress before, it can be an eye opener about whether you are effectively working toward the results you want. How does your list compare with where you thought you were on your journey?

Build a plan

What are all of the steps that need to happen before you can achieve your dream or goal? In the table below, list the major milestones that you need to reach on the way to making your dream or goal a reality—these are the signposts that will tell you that you're getting closer.

Milestone		What I need to do to achieve it
	🐾	
	🐾	
	🐾	
	🐾	
	🐾	
	🐾	
	🐾	
	🐾	
	🐾	
	🐾	

What's the difference between a goal and a dream? Your perceived likelihood of success. A goal is something you believe you can achieve one day if you keep working hard at it. A dream is something you don't necessarily think will ever happen, but you strongly believe achieving it would make you very happy.

Track your progess

Buy a journal or notebook to track your progress toward your goal.

Each time you take a step toward your next milestone, record the date and what you did. Also write down your setbacks, so that you have a record of what didn't work and why your goal may be taking longer than expected.

Whenever you reach a milestone, highlight it with a bright color. This will make it easy to spot your milestones when you look back at your progress. Under each milestone you achieve, write a short reflection on how you feel about getting to that point.

Even if you don't end up achieving your original goal or dream, look back through your journal to recognize everything you have experienced and learned from the process. What did you enjoy doing? How could you incorporate those things into your life in a different way, or create a new goal that involves the parts you enjoyed most on this journey?

Milestone: _____ Date: _____

What I did: _____
_____
_____
_____
_____
_____

How I felt: _____
_____
_____
_____
_____
_____
_____
_____
_____
_____
_____
_____
_____
_____

Be as Happy as Your Dog
15. Curl up and sleep

Sleep is your time for healing, rejuvenating, learning, de-stressing, understanding, and problem-solving. It is impossible to be happy without enough sleep.

How much do you sleep?

What time do you usually fall asleep (actually sleep, not just go to bed)?	
What time do you usually wake up?	
How many times do you typically wake up during the night, and for how long?	
Do you take any naps during the day? How many and for how long?	
Using your answers above, calculate how many hours of sleep do you typically get per day.	

If you are getting 7-8 hours of sleep per day and you feel rested, you are getting enough rest to maximize your potential for happiness. If you are getting less than this, I recommend continuing with the rest of this section.

Analyze your daily routine

Write down the steps you take during your evening routine, until the point where you fall asleep.

* When do you turn off your TV and other devices?
* When do you stop reading (if you read before bed) and turn out the light?
* What chores do you do before bedtime?
* What rituals do you have (e.g., brushing your teeth, stretching, journaling, etc.)?
* How long do you lie in bed before you fall asleep? What do you think about during this time?

1. _____

2. _____

3. _____

4. _____

5. _____

6. _____

7. _____

8. _____

What do you do in the morning after you wake up and before you leave the house or start your at-home day? How much time do you spend on things like choosing an outfit, showering and doing your hair and makeup, childcare, checking emails or messages, making breakfast(s), making lunch(es), etc.?

Take back your time

Make a plan to help you sleep more by streamlining some of your chores or changing your habits to improve your sleep. For example, turning off electronics earlier, going to bed at a consistent time, avoiding caffeine and alcohol in the evenings, reducing your grooming, doing weekly meal prep, carpooling your kids' school drop-off so you don't do it every morning, etc.

Time stealer	How I will change it

Modern society values being constantly busy and labels sleep as wasted time when nothing gets accomplished. Nothing could be further from the truth.

Improve your sleep

If you have trouble falling asleep, try some of these suggestions and keep track of which ones seem to help. You'll need to try things for at least a couple of weeks before you can tell whether they are helping you sleep, so choose one at a time and be patient. Add your own ideas to the list.

Technique		Results
Journaling before bedtime		
Writing a to-do list for tomorrow		
Using earplugs		
Using blackout curtains or blinds		
Listening to white noise or relaxing sounds		
Meditating before bedtime		
Doing breathing exercises in bed		
Stretching before bedtime		
Taking a hot bath in the evening		
Writing down things I'm grateful for		

16. Dig deeper

Sometimes, to figure out why happiness is a challenge for you, you need to dig below your surface feelings to find the root of your issues. Heal your roots so that you can bloom into happiness.

Find your why

Write down three things you think would make you truly happy if you had them or achieved them. Then take a moment to think about *why* you believe each one would make you happy. What is the underlying need or desire you think it would fulfill?

I would be truly happy if...

It would make me happy because...

I would be truly happy if...

It would make me happy because...

I would be truly happy if...

It would make me happy because...

Is there anything on your list that, upon reflection, you've decided would probably not make you happy because the underlying need or desire would still be there? Are there other ways you can think of to fulfill your needs and desires if the things on your list don't happen?

Barriers to happiness

List the issues preventing you from feeling happy (strained relationships, anxieties, traumas, fears, frustrations, etc.). After each one, name a person (or people) you could discuss each issue with to explore why it is holding you back. It could be someone who is directly involved, someone who knows you well, or a professional therapist, coach, counsellor, or other outside person. Use another sheet if need to.

Issue: Who can help:

Issue: Who can help:

Issue: Who can help:

Issue: Who can help:

Issue: Who can help:

Issue: Who can help:

Dig and heal

Outline steps you could take to help you understand and resolve the feelings that are stopping you from being happy. These could involve
- reconciling with people,
- removing people from your life,
- breaking a habit or stopping a behavior pattern,
- accepting yourself as you are,
or any other action that will help you move past your challenges and enjoy your life more. (Use separate sheets for multiple challenges if you need to.)

1. _____

2. _____

3. _____

4. _____

5. _____

6. _____

7. _____

8. _____

9. _____

10. _____

Look at your goals and activities and ask yourself why you have chosen to do those things. Are you trying to meet society's expectations or please others instead of doing what will make you happier?

Be as Happy as Your Dog
Stay pawsitive!

Notes

_____

_____

_____

_____

_____

_____

_____

_____

_____

_____

_____

_____

_____

_____

_____

_____

_____

_____

_____

_____

_____

_____

_____

Make a list of a few things you can start doing immediately to make you happier. Maybe it's going to bed earlier, adding more playtime to your schedule, savoring more positive experiences, or stopping to "smell" things more often. Whatever suggestions appeal to you most are the ones you're most likely to stick with.

_____

_____

_____

_____

_____

_____

_____

_____

_____

_____

_____

_____

Finding new ways to have more positive thoughts and dwell less on negative thoughts is the only way to increase your happiness. Looking at the world through a dog's eyes (and nose) can show us pathways to happiness that apply to two-leggers like you and me.

For media or speaking requests, permissions, or bulk purchases, contact the author at contact@beashappyasyourdog.com.

Published 2024, 1st edition

Cover photo: Samantha Rose Photography
Cover design: Michelle Fairbanks for Fresh Design; Michelle Waitzman

Subjects (BISAC): SELF-HELP—Personal Growth—Happiness; SELF-HELP—Motivational & Inspirational; PSYCHOLOGY-Positive Psychology

ISBN: 978-1-7387874-3-2

Also available:
Be as Happy as Your Dog: 16 Dog-Tested Ways to Be Happier Using Pawsitive Psychology
Paperback ISBN: 978-1-7387874-0-1
E-book ISBN: 978-1-7387874-1-8

Visit beashappyasyourdog.com for more information and buying options.